Bernhard Cossmann

1822 – 1910

Cello-Studies

Violoncello-Studien
Études pour le Violoncelle

for the suppleness and stamina of the fingers and the purity of intonation
für die Gefügigkeit der Finger und die Reinheit der Intonation
destinées à assouplir et portifier les doigts et la pureté de l'intonation

Edited by / Herausgegeben von / Edité par
Martin Müller-Runte

ED 964
ISMN 979-0-001-03232-2

www.schott-music.com

Mainz · London · Berlin · Madrid · New York · Paris · Prague · Tokyo · Toronto
© 1912/2008 SCHOTT MUSIC GmbH & Co. KG, Mainz · Printed in Germany

Vorwort

Bernhard Cossmann (1822 – 1910) war ein bekannter Solist und Lehrer. Er studierte bei Theodore Müller (Braunschweig), Karl Drechsler (Dessau) und Friedrich August Kummer (Dresden). Mit 18 Jahren wurde er Solocellist der Pariser Italienischen Oper, begann eine intensive Konzerttätigkeit in Deutschland, England und Irland und war Solist im Gewandhaus Orchester Leipzig unter Felix Mendelssohn Bartholdy. Freundschaften verbanden ihn u. a. mit Franz Liszt und dem Cellisten Alfredo Piatti. (Alfred Piatti hat seine 12 Capricen op. 25 Bernhard Cossmann gewidmet.)

Seine intensive Lehrtätigkeit führte ihn über Leipzig und das Moskauer Konservatorium nach Frankfurt am Main an das Hochsche Konservatorium. Er war nicht nur ein gefragter Solist und Lehrer, sondern trat auch als Komponist in Erscheinung und schrieb viele Solowerke für das Violoncello. Unter anderem arrangierte er auch Schuberts Erlkönig für Violoncello Solo, schrieb die *Fünf Neuen Concert Etüden*, die *Concert-Studien* (Alfred Piatti gewidmet), drei *Fantasien für Violoncello* über Themen aus Opern von Carl Maria von Weber (Wilhelm Tell, Euryanthe, Freischütz) und zahlreiche technische Studien.

Die hier neu vorgelegten Violoncello-Studien beinhalten gezielte Übungen für die Entwicklung der linken Hand wie Doppelgriff-Trillerstudien, Geläufigkeitsübungen, Akkordstudien, Tonleiterstudien sowie Daumenaufsatzstudien, die speziell den Einsatz des 4. Fingers intensiv mit einbeziehen. Als Extrakt spieltechnischer Anforderungen für die linke Hand sind diese Violoncello-Studien eine sinnvolle und hilfreiche Ergänzung zu der Etüdenliteratur des 18./19. Jahrhunderts mit den Werken von Dotzauer, Duport, Grützmacher, Romberg, Piatti und anderen.

Die Etüden wenden sich an den fortgeschrittenen Schüler, Studenten, aber auch an den fertig ausgebildeten Cellisten, der in knappen Übungen die Spielfertigkeit und Geläufigkeit der linken Hand entwickeln oder erhalten möchte.

Martin Müller-Runte

Themenübersicht

Préface

Bernhard Cossmann (1822 – 1910) était un soliste et enseignant de renom. Il fit ses études auprès de Theodore Müller (Brunswick), Karl Drechsler (Dessau) et Friedrich August Kummer (Dresde). A 18 ans, il devint violoncelliste soliste de l'Opéra italien de Paris, commença une activité de concerts intense en Allemagne, en Angleterre et en Irlande, et fut soliste à l'Orchestre du Gewandhaus de Leipzig sous la direction de Felix Mendelssohn Bartholdy. Il était lié d'amitié entre autres avec Franz Liszt et le violoncelliste Alfredo Piatti. (Alfredo Piatti a dédié à Bernhard Cossmann ses 12 caprices op. 25.)

Ses nombreuses missions d'enseignant le menèrent tout d'abord à Leipzig et au Conservatoire de Moscou, puis à Francfort s./Main au Conservatoire Hoch. Soliste et enseignant très demandé, il se fit connaître également en tant que compositeur, écrivant de nombreuses œuvres pour violoncelle solo. Il arrangea entre autres le *Roi des Aulnes* de Schubert pour le violoncelle solo, écrivit les *Cinq nouvelles études de concertos*, les *Etudes de concertos* (dédiées à Alfredo Piatti), trois *Fantaisies pour violoncelle* sur des thèmes des opéras de Carl Maria von Weber (*Guillaume Tell*, *Euryanthe*, *Le Freischütz*), et de nombreuses études techniques.

Les études pour violoncelle rééditées ici contiennent des exercices ciblés pour le développement de la main gauche, par exemple des études de trilles à doubles cordes, des études de vélocité, d'accords, de gammes, ainsi que des études de placement du pouce sur le manche, intégrant de manière particulièrement intense l'utilisation du quatrième doigt. Condensé d'exigences techniques de la main gauche, ces études pour violoncelle constituent un complément judicieux et utile à la littérature d'études des XVIIIème et XIVème siècles comportant les œuvres de Dotzauer, Duport, Grützmacher, Romberg, Piatti et autres.

Ces études s'adressent à des élèves et étudiants avancés, mais aussi au violoncelliste ayant achevé sa formation et désirant élaborer plus avant ou maintenir par des exercices succincts l'agilité et la vélocité de la main gauche.

Martin Müller-Runte
Traduction Martine Paulauskas

Sommaire

Preface

Bernhard Cossmann (1822 – 1910) was well known both as a soloist and as a teacher. He studied with Theodore Müller in Braunschweig, Karl Drechsler in Dessau and Friedrich August Kummer in Dresden. At the age of eighteen he was appointed principal cellist at the Italian Opera in Paris and embarked on a busy concert career, performing in Germany, England and Ireland and appearing as a soloist with the Gewandhaus Orchestra in Leipzig under Felix Mendelssohn Bartholdy. Franz Liszt and the cellist Alfredo Piatti were among his friends (Alfred Piatti dedicated his Twelve Caprices Op. 25 to Bernhard Cossmann).

Cossmann's teaching career took him to Leipzig, to the Moscow Conservatoire and to the Hoch Academy in Frankfurt am Main. Besides being in demand as a soloist and teacher, he also made a name for himself as a composer and wrote many solo works for the cello. Cossmann arranged Schubert's *Erlkönig* for cello solo, wrote Five New Concert Studies, a set of Concert Studies dedicated to Alfred Piatti, three Fantasias for the Cello based on themes from operas by Carl Maria von Weber (*Wilhelm Tell, Euryanthe, der Freischütz*) and numerous technical studies.

The Cello Studies in this new edition include exercises devised specifically to develop strength in the left hand, as well as trill exercises using double stopping, exercises in rapid articulation and studies in playing chords, scales and using thumb positions, with special emphasis on developing the use of the fourth finger. As a concise summary of techniques required for the left hand, these cello studies offer a useful and helpful addition to the repertoire of studies from the 18th and 19th Centuries in pieces by Dotzauer, Duport, Grützmacher, Romberg, Piatti and others.

These studies are designed for advanced students, but also for trained cellists looking for concise exercises to develop or maintain precise coordination and technical facility in the left hand.

Martin Müller-Runte
Translation Julia Rushworth

Topics covered

A

Trillerstudien

Études pour les trilles · Trill Studies

4

Der dritte Finger bleibt liegen · Le troisième doigt reste sur la corde · Keep the third finger down

Der zweite Finger bleibt liegen · Le deuxième doigt reste sur la corde · Keep the third finger down

Die bisherigen Übungen abwechselnd in den höheren Lagen (bis zur vierten Lage inkl.) und auf den tieferen Saiten

Exécuter les études précédentes dans les registres supérieurs (jusqu'a la quatrième position incl.) et sur les cordes graves

Play the foregoing studies alternately in the higher positions (up to and including fourth position) and on the lower strings

IV.

10

B
Akkordstudien
Études pour les accords · Chord Studies

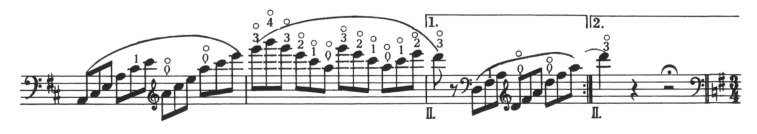

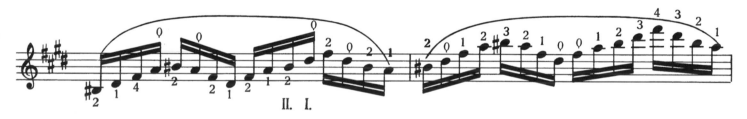

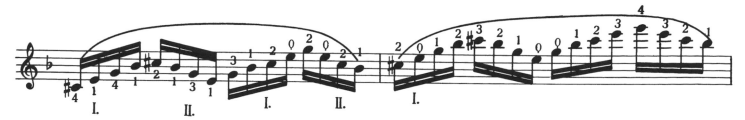

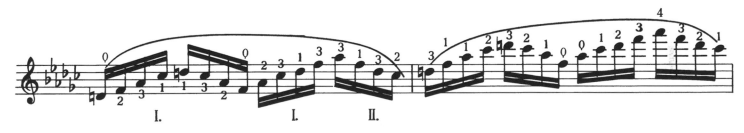

C

Skalenstudien

Études pour les gammes · Scale Studies

Zwei bis drei Bogen auf jede Tonleiter, nach der mehr
oder minder schnellen Ausführung zu bemessen

Donner deux ou trois coups d'archet pour
chaque gamme, selon la rapidité d'exécution

Take two or three bows per
scale, depending on your speed

①

23

D

Studien im Daumenaufsatz mit häufiger Anwendung des vierten Fingers
Études pour l'application du pouce avec utilisation fréquente du quartième doigt
Thumb studies with frequent use of the fourth finger

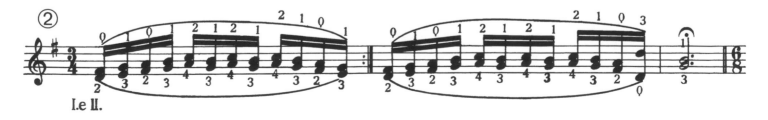

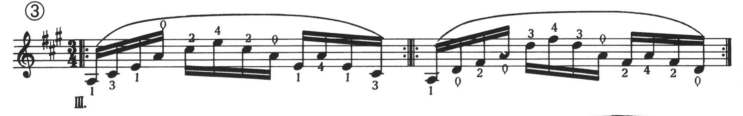

Die Übungen mit liegenbleibendem
Daumen abwechselnd in anderen Lagen

Jouer successivement en changeant de position
les études pour le maintien du pouce

Play the studies with the thumb down
alternately in other positions

hauptsächlich zu spielen zwischen   und
principalement entre · especially from   et · to

Schott Music, Mainz 22 075

Zeitgenössische Musik für Violoncello
Contemporary cello music
Musique contemporaine pour violoncelle

Violoncello solo
Cello solo
Violoncelle seule

Lucio Amanti
Jazz Suite
CB 224

Mikhail Bukinik
4 Konzertetüden
CB 179

Wolfgang Fortner
Suite
ED 2255
Thema und Variationen
ED 6635

Hans Werner Henze
Capriccio
ED 7279
Serenade
ED 4330
Sieben Liebeslieder
Solostimme
ED 7418

Paul Hindemith
Sonate, op. 25/3
ED 1979

Heinz Holliger
Chaconne
ED 6689
Trema
AVV 124

Klaus Huber
Transpositio ad Infinitum
ED 6684

Bertold Hummel
Abschied
CB 176

Christian Jost
lautlos
CB 185

Volker David Kirchner
Und Salomo sprach...
ED 7641

Gabriel Koeppen
Blues Time
3 Blues Pieces
ED 21243

György Ligeti
Sonate
ED 7698

Enrico Mainardi
Ballata della Lontonanza
ED 5763
Sette Preludi
ED 5492

Krzysztof Penderecki
Capriccio per Siegfried Palm
ED 6072
Per Slava
ED 7538

Aribert Reimann
Solo für Violoncello
ED 7099
Solo II für Violoncello
CB 172

Joaquín Rodrigo
Como una fantasía
CB 136

Dieter Schnebel
Fünf Inventionen
ED 7748

Violoncello und Klavier
Cello and piano
Violoncelle et piano

Lucio Amanti
Jazz Sonata
CB 231

Gavin Bryars
The North Shore
ED 12926
The South Downs
ED 12588

Georges Enescu
Nocturne et Saltarello
CB 168

Jindřich Feld
Sonate
CB 121

Wolfgang Fortner
Zyklus
ED 5436

Jean Françaix
Mouvement perpétuel
BSS 37704
Sérénade
BSS 37855

Harald Genzmer
1. Sonate
ED 4603

George Gershwin
Short Story
CB 126

Alexander Goehr
Fantasie, op. 77
ED 12869
Sonata, op. 45
ED 12256

Hans Werner Henze
Englische Balladen und Sonette
CB 174

Kurt Hessenberg
Sonate C-Dur, op. 23
ED 3785

Paul Hindemith
A frog he went a-courting
ED 4276
Meditation aus „Nobilissima Visione"
ED 3685
Kleine Sonate
ED 8186

Sonate, op. 11/3
ED 1986
Sonate
ED 3839

Thomas Larcher
Mumien
CB 182

Enrico Mainardi
Sonata
ED 4678
Sonata quasi fantasia
ED 5459

Aribert Reimann
Sonate
AVV 16

Joaquín Rodrigo
Sonata a la breve
CB 137

Alexander Rosenblatt
Blues
CB 227
Jazz Sonata
CB 228

Nikolaj Andrejewitsch Roslawez
1. Sonate
ED 8038
2. Sonate
ED 8039

Erwin Schulhoff
Sonate
CB 151

István Szelényi
Aria
ED 9488

Toru Takemitsu
Orion
SJ 1019

Ernst Toch
Sonate, op. 50
ED 2084

Mark-Anthony Turnage
Sleep On
3 Lullabies
ED 12447
Two Vocalises
ED 12840

Huw Watkins
Sonata
ED 12854

Bernd Alois Zimmermann
Intercomunicazione
ED 6004

2 und mehr Violoncelli
2 and more cellos
2 et plus violoncelles

Lucio Amanti
Jazz Duets
ED 21598

Werner Egk
Quartetto per violoncelli
CB 180

Jean Françaix
Aubade
für 12 Violoncelli
Partitur ED 6710
Stimmensatz ED 6794
Scuola di Celli
Suite von zehn Stücken
für 10 Violoncelli
Partitur ED 8034
Stimmensatz ED 7784

Hans Werner Henze
Trauer-Ode
für 6 Violoncelli
CB 166

Paul Hindemith
Duett
für 2 Violoncelli
ED 8338

Vytautas Laurušas
Concento di corde
per due violoncelli
CB 181

Gerd Natschinski
Pas de deux nostalgiques
für 4 Violoncelli
CB 188

Eduard Pütz
Blues Fantasy
für 6 Violoncelli
CB 165
Sonata
Für 7 Violoncelli
CB 173
Tango Passionato
Für 4 Violoncelli
CB 159

Rodion Shchedrin
Hamlet Ballad
für 4 Violoncelli
CB 178

Friedrich K. Wanek
7 Aphorismen
für 2 Violoncelli
CB 154

Friedrich Zehm
Moderne Tänze
für 2 Violoncelli
CB 128

SCHOTT
www.schott-music.com

R 316-5-13